# I Think I Might Be Autistic

*A Guide to Autism Spectrum Disorder Diagnosis and
Self-discovery for Adults*

by

Cynthia Kim

Narrow
Gauge

MAY - - 2015
CH

ISBN 978-0-9895971-1-1

**Disclaimer**

This book is designed to provide information about autism spectrum disorder. It is not the purpose of this book to reprint all the information that is otherwise available to the author, publisher, printer or distributors, but instead to complement, amplify and supplement other texts. You are urged to read available material, learn as much as you wish about the subjects covered in this book and tailor the information to your individual needs.

Every effort has been made to make this book as complete and accurate as possible. However, there may be mistakes, both typographical and in content. Therefore, this text should be used only as a general guide and not as the ultimate source of information on the subjects presented. The authors, publisher, printer and distributors shall neither have liability nor responsibility to any person or entity with respect to loss or damages caused, or alleged to have been caused, directly or indirectly, by the information contained in this book. If you do not wish to be bound by the above, you may return this book to the publisher for a full refund.

# Contents

# 1

# Introduction

When I first suspected I might have Asperger's syndrome, my instinct was to look for something—a test or a book or a website—that would confirm or disprove my suspicion. I spent hours and then days searching the internet for the type of resource I imagined must be out there.

I found plenty of information about identifying autism and Asperger's in children, but very little for adults. "Well," I thought, "I guess I'll just have to get some sort of professional evaluation." I figured it would be like getting diagnosed with any other health condition: I'd visit my doctor, he'd refer me to a specialist, the specialist would do some tests and offer me a definitive answer to my question: *Am I autistic?*

That was the beginning of a year-long quest, which ultimately resulted in an Asperger's Syndrome diagnosis. Along the way I discovered that not only was it challenging to get an autism assessment as an adult, there was very little information available to guide adults like me through the process.

Compounding the lack of resources, many general practitioners and mental health professionals are unfamiliar with how autism looks in an adult. The first professional I asked about getting an assessment—a university mental health counselor—looked at me like I had three heads. Then she made a half dozen phone calls and, unable to refer me to anyone in the community, shuffled me off to the university's disability resource center with an apology.

Adults who suspect they may be on the autism spectrum often need to become self-advocates, arming themselves with the information necessary to "make their case" to a series of medical professionals.

When I began blogging, I quickly realized that I wasn't alone in how difficult I found navigating the medical and mental health system. Many of the comments I received on my blog were from adults in their twenties, thirties, forties and fifties who were beginning to suspect they might be aspie or autistic. There were a range of reactions from relief and happiness to panic and despair. Many asked me how I confirmed that I have Asperger's. Others described long, complicated journeys through the mental health system fraught with misdiagnoses. Some said they'd given up and were content with their own well-researched self-diagnosis or with an informal diagnosis received in the course of therapy or from their autistic child's psychologist.

One theme that ran through so many of those "I think I might be autistic" comments was how each person felt that he or she had to figure out the diagnostic process from start to finish. This struck me as not only highly inefficient but unnecessary.

By that point, I'd struggled through the process from those earliest realizations to receiving my official looking diagnostic report. I'd read dozens of other autistic adults' experiences with getting or trying to get a diagnosis. Thanks to my newly developed special interest in autism, I had a strong foundation of knowledge. Putting all of those things together, I began to develop a blog post about getting diagnosed with autism spectrum disorder as an adult.

And this is where I should qualify everything you're about to read by saying: I'm not a medical professional. I'm an autistic adult who has done a lot of research about autism. I write from personal experience and have done my best to fact check my research but this guide is by no means all-inclusive or infallible. I strongly recommend that you do as much additional research as necessary to make the choices that you feel are appropriate to your situation.

With that out of the way, let's get started.

What follows is background information, tips and suggestions for adults who think they might be autistic mixed with a personal account of my own discovery and diagnosis process. I hope it strikes a balance of encouragement and caution. My Asperger's diagnosis was one of the best things that ever happened to me, but getting to that day when the diagnostic report arrived in the mail wasn't always easy.

My goal in writing this isn't to tell you what to do, but to show you what worked and didn't work for me and provide you with the knowledge and resources you'll need to make your own way through the discovery and diagnosis process.

*A note on language: The language used to talk about autism spectrum disorders can be confusing at first.*

*I use autism, autism spectrum disorder and Asperger's syndrome interchangeably. Asperger's syndrome is no longer an official diagnosis in the United States, having been folded into autism spectrum disorder as of May 2013. People who were diagnosed before Asperger's syndrome was retired are still regarded as having Asperger's, even though today they would be diagnosed with autism spectrum disorder.*

*I also use autistic and aspie (shorthand for a person who has Asperger's syndrome) interchangeably to refer to myself. I sometimes use person "with autism", "on the autism spectrum" or "with Asperger's" when it makes the text easier to read. There is no single correct term. When referring to a specific person, it's always best to inquire if they have a preference and then use it.*

# Autism Spectrum Disorder: Definition and Traits

If you're reading this, you may already have a good idea of what autism spectrum disorder is. However, due to the way autism is commonly portrayed in popular culture, you may have some misconceptions as well. I know I did.

Let's start with a definition of autism spectrum disorder, based on the American Psychology Association's Diagnostic and Statistical Manual of Mental Disorders Fifth Edition (DSM-5):

**Autism Spectrum Disorder (ASD):** This phrase describes a developmental disorder characterized by persistent lifelong impairments in social communication as well as the presence of restricted, repetitive patterns of behavior, interests or activities. These symptoms appear in early childhood, and may vary in intensity or manifestation throughout a person's lifetime. Taken together, symptoms of ASD impair and limit everyday functioning in some areas. Until May 2013, Asperger's Syndrome and Pervasive Development Disorder - Not Otherwise Specified (PDD-NOS) were treated as separate subtypes of ASD. This is no longer the case.

There are four specific and highly technical criteria for diagnosing ASD. I'm going to summarize them using technical language first for accuracy. Below that you'll find a list of questions in plain English to help you make sense of the technical definition.

The criteria for diagnosing autism spectrum disorder according to DSM-5 can be summarized as:

A. The presence of deficits in (1) social-emotional reciprocity (difficulty with back and forth conversation, approaching others socially, or limited/lack of social interaction), (2) nonverbal communication used for social interaction (atypical body language, eye contact, facial expression and/or gestures), and (3) developing and maintaining relationships (making age-appropriate friends, showing interest in people).

B. The presence of at least two of the following: (1) repetitive speech, movements or use of objects (also known as stimming), (2) excessive adherence to routines or patterns of behavior or excessive resistance to change, (3) interests that are abnormal in intensity or focus, (4) hyper- or hypo-reactivity to sensory input or unusual interest in sensory aspects of the environment.

C. Symptoms must have been present from early childhood. Symptoms from category A must be present at the time of diagnosis. Symptoms from category B must have been present in childhood, but do not need to be present during adulthood in the case of adult diagnosis.

D. Symptoms limit and impair everyday functioning.

In summary, for a clinical diagnosis of ASD, you need to have all 3 symptoms from criteria A, 2 from criteria B, and you must meet the conditions of both C and D.

Unless you're trained in autism assessment or have done extensive reading about ASD, much of the jargon in the official diagnostic criteria isn't very meaningful. To help you sort out which symptoms you experience, I've developed a simple list of questions for each of the symptom groups. A "yes" answer to a question indicates that you have a trait or behavior in common with many autistic adults.

There is no minimum number of questions that you need to answer affirmatively to qualify as having a symptom. And not everyone experiences these traits in the same way. I might answer "yes" to an entirely different set of questions than another autistic adult, but that doesn't mean that one of us is more autistic or less autistic than the other. The key word in "autism spectrum disorder" is *spectrum*: we are a diverse group of individuals, with varied life experiences as well as differing symptom clusters.

An ASD diagnosis is, ultimately, a judgment call made by a professional with a great deal of experience in making such calls. The questions that follow are simply a guide to help you understand how autistic traits can appear in adults (and older teens).

## A1: Difficulties with social initiation and response

1. Do you find it hard to approach others to initiate a conversation?

2. Do you have difficulty entering into a social group or conversation?

3. Do you struggle with knowing when it's your turn to talk?

4. Do you frequently interrupt others or leave unusually long pauses in conversations?

5. Do you find yourself having one-sided conversations in which you're doing most of the talking?

6. Do you get easily bored when someone wants to talk about a subject that doesn't interest you?

7. Do you find it difficult to engage in "small talk"?

8. Do you see conversations as primarily a way to exchange information rather than emotionally connect with people?

9. Do you find it hard to explain something in a different way if someone doesn't understand you the first time?

10. Do you find it hard to get excited when someone else shares news of an exciting or enjoyable experience they had?

11. Does praise make you uncomfortable because you're unsure how to respond?

12. Do you find that you don't enjoy social interactions in the way others seem to enjoy them?

13. Do you have an aversion to physical affection or other types of typically pleasurable physical contact?

14. Do you find it difficult to ask for help from others?

## A2: Difficulties with nonverbal communication

1.  Do you have trouble coordinating eye contact and gestures or other body language during conversation?

2.  Have you been told that your facial expressions are inappropriate for the situation or do not match your feelings?

3.  Have others told you that your facial expressions often look angry, depressed or blank, even when you don't feel that way?

4.  Have you been told that you stare at people inappropriately?

5.  Do you have difficulty smiling for photos or otherwise putting on an appropriate facial expression "on demand"?

6.  Do you find making eye contact uncomfortable, difficult or even painful?

7.  When talking with others, do you tend to look or face away from them under certain conditions, such as when you're thinking or when the

conversation becomes emotionally intense?

8.  Have you been told that you often speak too loudly, too softly or too quickly to be easily understood?

9.  Do you find yourself imitating the accents or speech patterns of the person you are talking to?

10. Have you been told that your speech is flat or monotonous?

11. Have others described you as cold, detached, or bored when you weren't feeling that way?

12. Do you have difficulty reading other people's facial expressions or body language?

13. Do you have difficulty recognizing sarcasm?

## A3. Difficulties with relationships

1.  Do you find it difficult to judge how another person is feeling about you?

2.  Do you have trouble judging how another person is reacting to your words or actions?

3.  Do you often miss social cues that others seem to easily understand?

4.  Do you laugh or smile at the wrong time?

5.  Have you been told that you're aloof, withdrawn or in your own world?

6.  Do you have a lower than average need for social interaction?

7. Do you often prefer solitary activities or spending time alone?

8. Do you find interacting with people who are much younger or much older than you easier than interacting with your same-age peers?

9. Do you find it difficult to make new friends?

10. Do you struggle with maintaining friendships?

11. Do you prefer to have just one or two close friends at a time?

12. Do you wish you had more friends but don't know how to establish friendships?

13. Do you have distant or strained relationships with family members, especially for reasons that you find hard to understand?

14. Do you find it hard to tell if someone is teasing or mocking you?

15. Do you have trouble figuring out when someone wants you to do something if they don't specifically tell you? (example: saying they're cold and wanting you to offer them a blanket or sweater)

16. Do you prefer one-on-one interaction over group interaction?

17. Do you sometimes avoid or ignore people who want to interact with you?

18. Do you find it hard to understand the unwritten rules of social interaction?

19. Do you rely on scripted speech or imitating others in social situations?

20. Do you have difficulty reacting in expected ways to another person's distress?

21. Do you find it hard to judge when it's okay to join in a group activity or conversation?

22. Do others tell you that you're insensitive or that you don't seem to notice their feelings?

23. Do others call you selfish because you only seem to be thinking of yourself in certain situations?

24. Are you often surprised when another person tells you what they were thinking after you've had a misunderstanding?

### B1. Atypical speech and movements

1. Do you repeat sounds such as animal sounds, grunts, growls or hums?

2. Do you repeat words, phrases or longer passages of speech that you've heard, such as from a movie or conversation partner? (either immediately or a long time after hearing the original speech)

3. Do you have a large vocabulary or a strong preference for very exact use of words, regardless of how commonly used those words might be?

4. Do you use unusually formal words or speech structure?

5. Do you have some phrases that you use frequently,

even when they're not exactly appropriate?

6. Do you use a lot of metaphors, especially ones that you've made up (that might not make sense to others)?

7. Are there aspects of your speech content or structure that others find hard to understand until they get to know you?

8. Do you refer to yourself by your name instead of using "I"?

9. Do you have difficulty referring to others by name?

10. Do you ever confuse "I" and "you" (or other non-gendered pronouns) in speech?

11. Do you sometimes feel the need to repeatedly talk about the same subject, even when the other person has asked you to stop or is no longer listening?

12. Do you perform repetitive hand movements like flapping your hands, flicking your fingers or manipulating an object with your fingers?

13. Do you perform repetitive whole body movements like rocking, bouncing, walking on your toes, skipping, spinning or swaying?

14. Do you repeatedly pick at your skin or scalp?

15. Do you like to sit, stand or otherwise position yourself in unusual ways, such as curling up in small spaces or lying/sitting with certain body

parts under you?

16. Do you grind your teeth or bite your lips or cheek excessively?

17. Have you been told that you make unusual facial expressions (grimacing, flinching, etc.) repeatedly, often without realizing it?

18. Do you enjoy using objects in ways other than how they were intended? (examples: twirling a piece of string, chewing on objects, repeatedly opening and closing things, lining up or arranging things by color or category)

## B2: Rituals and resistance to change

1. Do you sometimes feel the need to repeatedly ask the same questions even after your question has been answered?

2. Do you need to say a particular thing in a certain way at certain times or have other people always answer certain questions in specific ways?

3. Do you have compulsive behaviors, like always touching the door jamb before entering a room or brushing your hair for exactly 50 strokes before getting in the shower?

4. Do you find it hard to understand certain types of humor?

5. Do you have difficulty understanding nonliteral types of speech such as irony, sarcasm, symbolism or allusions?

6. Do you find it difficult to end one activity and begin another?

7. Do you struggle to begin or complete self-care tasks, even when you know that a task is essential or overdue?

8. Do other people tell you that you sometimes overreact to small changes in plans or your environment? (even if you don't consider the changes small)

9. Do you have a lot of routines that you rely on to get through the day or to navigate certain situations?

10. Do you get upset when someone or something disrupts one of your routines?

11. Do you have routines that other people think are unusual or that no one else seems to do?

12. Have you been told that your thinking is "black and white" or "all or nothing"?

13. Do you have trouble seeing other people's point of view in a discussion or argument?

14. Do you find it hard to apologize or admit that you're wrong after you've taken a strong stance in a discussion?

15. Do you have a lot of rules that you like to follow?

16. Do you expect others to follow your rules?

17. Do other people tell you that you're controlling or bossy?

18. Do you get frustrated by things that aren't clearly defined? (for example, when someone insists on answering "well, it depends on the situation" or when there is no clear answer to a problem)

19. Do you find open-ended questions hard to answer?

20. Do you have trouble changing your mind or adjusting your plans if you're presented with new information or a situation suddenly changes?

## B3: Intense or unusual interests

1.  Do you tend to get obsessed with certain topics, sometimes for reasons you can't explain?

2.  When you're interested in a topic, does it seem to take over many aspects of your life? (examples: you find yourself talking, thinking and reading about it, collecting and making things related to it, relating many diverse aspects of your life to it)

3.  Do you have an object that you like to have with you at all times, especially something that's unusual for your age?

4.  Do you find that you naturally focus more on the details of things than on the whole? (for example, when you walk into a new coffee shop, you might notice a sign then a person then a pattern on the wall then the sound of the espresso machine rather than immediately perceiving where you need to go to order your coffee)

5. Do you have interests that are unusually intense compared to your peers? (for example, you're a college student majoring in math but you are as well-versed in seventeenth century Italian opera as a music professor specializing in the subject)

6. Do you have highly unusual interests? (for example, are you intensely interested in methods for training champion fighting beetles or do you the have world's largest cigar band collection?)

7. Do you have a narrow range of interests?

8. Does your leisure time always focus on just one or two activities or topics?

9. Do you have a passion for numbers, letters, words or symbols, including individual specimens (such as the number 3) or categories (such as primes)?

10. Do you consider yourself or have you been told that you're a perfectionist?

11. Do you like to collect and/or categorize items?

12. Do you have large collections of factual knowledge, particularly in a specific category like dates, models, statistics or systems?

## B4: Atypical sensory experiences

1. Do you prefer certain textures and/or find certain textures hard to tolerate?

2. Do you find that textures, features or styles of clothing (e.g., tags, seams, high/tight collar or

waists) that don't seem to bother other people are irritating or even upsetting to you?

3. Do you find showers, haircuts or other common self-care tasks physically uncomfortable or painful?

4. Are you unusually sensitive to light touch on your skin?

5. Do you notice physical sensations that others don't seem to notice, such as the feeling of air moving in an air conditioned room?

6. Are you unusually sensitive to heat or cold?

7. Are you easily startled by loud sounds or do you find certain sounds painful?

8. Do you have unusually sensitive hearing?

9. Do you often hear sounds that others don't notice?

10. Do you have difficulty following conversations when there is a lot of background noise?

11. Do you find a certain type or intensity of light painful or otherwise hard to tolerate?

12. Are you unusually sensitive to specific smells, often to the point that if you can't escape them you'll become physically ill?

13. Do you find it impossible to eat certain types of foods due to their unpleasant taste or texture?

14. Do you sometimes become physically ill

(nauseous, dizzy, severe headache) around certain types of sensory input (e.g., fluorescent lights, sirens, strobes, machinery)?

15. Do you have an unusually high tolerance for pain?

16. Do you enjoy watching moving objects for extended periods of time?

17. Are you strongly drawn to certain smells or visual patterns?

18. Do you seek out certain types of movement like swinging, bouncing, speed, or flight?

19. Do you seek out deep pressure such as tight hugs, heavy blankets or tight spaces?

## C: Traits must be present in early childhood

1. Have most of your current traits been present since early childhood (age 8 and younger)? Keep in mind that traits may have been different in severity or type when you were younger. For example, in elementary school you had difficulty maintaining friendships because you were "too bossy" but as an adult you have difficulty because you struggle with social rules or prefer to spend time alone.

2. Are there some questions above that you can answer "yes" to when thinking about your childhood, even if those traits are no longer present today? This is especially important for B1-B4, where traits only need to be present in childhood for a diagnosis.

## D. Traits must limit and impair daily function

*Being limited and impaired is not the same as being completely unable to do something. Daily function includes: caring for yourself, performing manual tasks, seeing, hearing, eating, sleeping, speaking, learning, reading, concentrating, thinking, communicating, and working.*

Are any of the following true as a result of the traits identified in parts A and B:

1. Are you unemployed?

2. Do you find it difficult to keep a job, even one that you're well qualified for?

3. Are you underemployed (have substantially more training or education than is required for your job)?

4. To do your job, do you need supports or accommodations that other similarly qualified/trained co-workers don't require?

5. Do you have difficulty completing assignments or tests on time?

6. Are you unable to take clear or complete written notes from verbal instructions or lectures?

7. Do you often miss appointments or have unfinished tasks due to planning or organizational challenges?

8. Do you find it hard to keep up with self-care tasks like personal grooming, cooking, shopping and

cleaning?

9. Do you have difficulty scheduling your daily activities to the point that important tasks frequently don't get competed?

10. Do you often find that you miss deadlines or are unable to complete tasks necessary for living independently?

11. Are you unable to drive or utilize public transportation to get around as you need or would like to?

12. Do you have difficulty speaking or otherwise communicating with others?

13. Do you avoid going places or attending events, especially in new or unfamiliar settings?

14. Do you avoid meeting or interacting with people, especially in unstructured settings?

15. Do you have fewer friends than you'd ideally like to have?

16. Are you estranged from your family?

17. Do you wish you had a romantic partner but are unable to initiate or maintain romantic relationships?

18. Do you struggle with decision making?

19. Do you have uneven sets of skills? (e.g., you can comfortably speak in front of a large group at work but are unable to speak to a small group of strangers at a party?

The above is by no means an exhaustive inventory but it should give you an idea of the types of things autistic adults commonly experience. Some of these traits are similar to those experienced by autistic children, but there are also some traits that we tend to leave behind in childhood and others that are specific to the demands of adulthood.

When I originally started exploring the possibility of having Asperger's, the symptom lists I found were primarily aimed at parents of young children. Since I wasn't sitting around my living room spinning the wheels of my toy car for hours on end or licking the other kids at preschool, I figured I couldn't possibly be autistic. Now I know better. Just like all kids, autistic kids grow up and when we do, we look a little different than our younger brothers and sisters on the spectrum.

There is one more set of characteristics to consider—traits you won't find in diagnostic criteria but you will frequently hear autistic people talk about experiencing. In addition to formally recognized diagnostic criteria, many autistic people experience:

- insomnia or irregular sleeping patterns
- persistent anxiety
- impaired fine motor coordination: difficulty with tasks like tying shoes or holding a pencil
- impaired gross motor coordination: clumsiness at sports, bumping into stationary objects, etc.
- alexithymia: difficulty recognizing and/or talking about one's own emotions, difficulty differentiating between physical sensations

and emotions, difficulty recognizing the emotions of others
- prosopagnosia: faceblindness or difficulty recognizing familiar people, especially out of context
- meltdowns or shutdowns: periods of intense emotional upset, often characterized by uncontrollable crying, physical withdrawal from the surrounding environment and/or reduction in verbal skills, often followed by a period of intense fatigue
- auditory processing issues: difficulty understanding spoken language, often experienced as a delay between hearing spoken words and being able to process those audio sounds into recognizable words

## Common Terms Defined

As you read about autism spectrum disorder here and elsewhere, you'll come across some terms that may be unfamiliar. Here is a short list of definitions for commonly used words and phrases:

**Allistic:** This refers to someone who is not autistic.

**Asperger's Syndrome (AS):** Asperger's syndrome is an autism spectrum disorder characterized by deficits in social interaction together with behaviors, activities or interests that are repetitive or restricted. When it was a formal diagnosis (between 1981 and 2013) AS was generally differentiated from classical autism by the lack of a delay in language development. There is no longer a diagnostic distinction made based on language delay and AS is no longer given as a diagnosis since the publication of DSM-5. Furthermore, the recently released diagnostic guidelines state that a person previously diagnosed with Asperger's Syndrome should be given a diagnosis of autism spectrum disorder if they require an updated diagnosis under the DSM-5 criteria.

**Aspie**: An aspie is a person with Asperger's Syndrome.

**Central Coherence**: This refers to a person's ability to extract meaning or see "the big picture" in an information processing task. People with weak central coherence tend to focus on the details at the expense of the big picture (think of an essay that is grammatically perfect but has poor organization). People with strong central coherence tend to see the overall meaning while sacrificing details (the essay is well organized but riddled with typos and grammar errors).

**Executive Function**: Executive function is a catch-all term that includes our higher cognitive functions such as planning, working memory, attention, problem solving, verbal reasoning, inhibition, mental flexibility, multi-tasking, and initiation and monitoring of physical actions. Impaired executive function is a characteristic of ASD and one that many people continue to struggle with throughout adulthood.

**Neurotypical (NT)**: Neurotypical, a mash-up of the words neurologically typical, is often used as shorthand for people who are not on the spectrum, though nonautistic people can be neuro-atypical as well. A more correct term for nonautistic people is allistic.

**Perseverative**: This is a fancy word for repetitive. It's used to describe the repetitive actions, thoughts or speech of people with ASD. It can also refer to the tendency of people with autism to continue doing something the same way even though the task at hand has changed. You may also see perseveration (noun form) or perseverate (verb form).

**Pragmatics** (pragmatic use of language): Pragmatics refers to the social use of language. Autistic people often have difficulty with pragmatic use of language, particularly with interpreting nonverbal communication and the nuances of social interaction.

**Stimming**: Short for "self-stimulation" stimming refers to repetitive movements like rocking or hand waving. The technical term for these repetitive movements, which is used in the formal diagnostic criteria, is stereotypic movement or stereotypies (pronounced stare-ee-AH-tip-ees).

# 3

# I Think I Might Be Autistic. Now What?

So, you think you might be an aspie or autistic or somewhere on the autism spectrum. Now what?

First, take a deep breath. Relax. Nothing's changed. You're the same person you were before you took that test, read that article or had a light bulb go off while talking to someone about autism.

I remember my first inklings that I might be an aspie. I was listening to an NPR story about David Finch, the author of *The Journal of Best Practices*. His first hint that he had Asperger's was an online quiz that his wife asked him to take because she recognized so many aspie traits in him.

As he described the quiz questions, for the first time I realized that Asperger's Syndrome is more than social awkwardness and that I'm more than painfully shy. The symptoms that stood out most for me were the ones I'd never known were "symptoms" of anything other than my personality: attachment to routine, resistance to change, special interests, a need to be alone. Down the list I went, nodding and thinking *yes, yes, yes, ohmygoshyes*.

I went in search of the Aspie Quiz (http://rdos. net/eng/Aspie-quiz.php) and what really blew me away were the specific behavioral questions: Have you been accused of staring? Yes! Do you tend to talk too loudly or too softly? Yes! Do you have difficulty filtering out background noise? Yes!

How had I not seen this before?

I'd heard a similar interview with Finch back in 2009. *Interesting*, I'd thought at the time, but nothing more. I'd read quite a bit about autism, because I was drawn to the subject. It never occurred to me to ask why. I'd taken the Autism Spectrum Quotient (AQ) Test (http://www.wired.com/wired/archive/9.12/aqtest.html) several times in the past. Every single time I scored above the cutoff for being on the spectrum. Every single time I told myself that it was probably a fluke, or even more improbably, that most people likely scored that high.

For years I'd tiptoed around the subject of autism. Finally, at 42, I was ready to explore the possibility that I was autistic.

**Processing Your First Contact with Asperger's or Autism**

---

- Nothing has changed; everything has changed.
- Know that no matter how it feels right now, this can be a positive realization.
- If you're on the spectrum, learning more about what that means can help you understand yourself better and learn to cope more effectively with the challenges that an Autism Spectrum Disorder (ASD) presents.

---

# 4

# Paths to Realization

As an adult, there are a few common ways that you might realize you're on the spectrum:

- your child is diagnosed with ASD and in the process of learning more about autism, you recognize autistic traits in yourself
- someone in your life reads or hears about Asperger's or autism and tells you that they see a lot of ASD traits in you
- you hear or read about Asperger's or autism in the media and recognize yourself in the description of ASD traits
- you take one of the online ASD tests and get a result that says you are "likely an aspie" or "likely autistic"

Your reaction to this first contact with Asperger's or autism might be "I kind of knew that" or it might be "bullshit!"

For many years, I dismissed my AQ scores. I was convinced that everyone who took the test got a score that said they were likely autistic. Wouldn't everyone answer the way I did if they were being honest? Completely irrational, yes, but I wasn't ready to accept what was staring me in the face.

Then came the Finch story on NPR. When it was over, I Googled "Asperger's tests" and came upon the Aspie Quiz. My score was way above the cutoff for Asperger's. I took it again, answering more conservatively. Still above the cutoff.

I sat there at my desk for long minutes. Could it be possible that I've been autistic all my life and not known it? That was a stunning realization—one that would require me to reframe everything I thought I knew about myself and everything I'd assumed I knew about autism.

I've always known that I'm different. I've been labeled shy, weird, introverted, geeky. But what if I wasn't just weird? What if this thing called Asperger's explained everything about me that was different?

That was an exciting thought. If it was true, it gave me a whole new way of thinking about my life.

## Embracing Your Realization

---

- Relax. Breathe.
- Take some time to think about what being on the spectrum might mean to you.
- Retake the AQ or Aspie Quiz as many times as you need to.
- Make a list of traits that you see in yourself, including specific examples if you find it helpful.
- Reassure yourself that you aren't making this up.

---

# 5

## Is This Me?

I didn't do anything with my realization right away. It was a lot to process. I kept coming back to the possibility that I was imagining it.

Late the next day, during a long drive home with my husband, I brought up my suspicion that I might be an aspie. His reaction was guarded. He listened, agreed with much of what I said, then reassured me that he loves me exactly the way I am. It was a good discussion, but he didn't sound convinced. I needed more data to back up my hypothesis.

Back at home that night, I showed him some things online, including Rudy Simone's list of Female Asperger Syndrome Traits[1]. He read through the list, nodding at many of the traits, just as I had, looking a little more convinced of my hypothesis with each "hit."

In the days that followed, I searched the internet for more information about Asperger's and found frustratingly little that applied to adults. I felt like I needed a more comprehensive resource, something

---

1    You can find the list at (http://www.help4aspergers.com/ pb/wp_a58d4f6a/images/img244154ad237783e339.JPG) or by searching online for "Rudy Simone list of female asperger traits"

that would give me a better picture of Asperger's than the sometimes conflicting bits and pieces I was collecting online. (Sadly I hadn't yet discovered autistic bloggers who are an amazingly rich resource on what it is like to be an autistic adult.)

Determined to find more information about Asperger's for adults, I scoured the reviews at Amazon.com and settled on *The Complete Guide to Asperger's Syndrome* by Tony Attwood. Having now read a good portion of the books available on ASD, this is the still one book I'd recommend to anyone looking for an accessible, reasonably comprehensive starting place.

Attwood covers not only the types of traits that make up ASD, but how they affect us growing up and what we can do to compensate for some of the more challenging aspects of being on the spectrum. He doesn't focus exclusively on adult ASD but he includes more information for adults than most of the other general guides to autism, which tend to focus on autistic children.

Diving into Attwood's book immediately after it arrived on my doorstep, I spent hours underlining and annotating it. I read passages aloud to my husband. I made notes and looked up things like executive function and special interests online. Most of all, I just kept saying to myself, "This is me. I'm an aspie."

Somehow, it had taken me 42 years to recognize it.

## Gathering Information to Support your Realization

---

- Research autism spectrum disorder.
- Read about how autistic traits appear in adults.
- Read about the differences between autistic traits in men and women.
- Read personal narratives written by aspies and autistic individuals.
- When you feel ready, find a trusted person in your life who can give you an objective assessment of which traits they see in you.

---

# 6

# Autism as a Sensemaking Narrative

Working my way through *The Complete Guide to Asperger's Syndrome*, I found myself revisiting moments in my life that had been confusing, painful or traumatic. Suddenly, so much of my life made sense in the context of aspie traits.

Difficulty making friends? *Impaired social communication skills*

Clumsy? *Motor planning deficit*

Poor handwriting? *Problems with fine motor coordination*

Massive stamp/coin/doll/baseball card/lego collections? *Abnormally intense interests*

Not a hugger? *Tactile defensiveness*

The odd reactions I get from people? *Poor eye contact, flat affect, inability to read body language*

and on and on and on . . .

When I got to Attwood's description of the little aspie girl lining up her Barbie dolls and their clothes instead of playing with them, I literally shouted with joy. There are other people like me! I'm not defective. I'm not randomly weird. I'm an aspie. One of many.

I'd found my tribe and it was good.

This process of giving meaning to experiences is sometimes known as sensemaking or creating a sensemaking narrative. It happens when our current way of understanding ourselves or our situation is inadequate. Without the Asperger's piece of the puzzle, I was forced to cobble together incomplete explanations for my developmental history and my life experiences.

Once I had a basic understanding of Asperger's, I could apply that knowledge to "make sense of" my life in a new way.

Sensemaking has a few key steps, most of which I found happening naturally as I processed my newfound identity.

## The Sensemaking Process

1. **Shift in identity** - identification as aspie/autistic
2. **Retrospection** - looking back at key life events in the context of this new identity
3. **Building narrative accounts** - retelling the story of your life in light of AS/autism
4. **Sharing your narratives** - strengthening and preserving your stories by sharing them with others
5. **Reflecting** - the ongoing process of receiving feedback on your stories and reshaping them as your understanding of your narrative changes

Each person's sensemaking narrative is unique. Mine takes several forms: thought, speech and especially writing. My blog—including the thousands of comments from readers and my replies to them—is the cornerstone of my sensemaking narrative.

## Making Sense

---

- As you learn more about ASD, does it help you better understand difficult or confusing life events?
- Can you retell those events in a new way now?
- When you're ready, share your new understanding with trusted people in your life.
- Sharing can take many forms: oral, written, visual or mixed media. It can be factual, fictional, derivative or a combination. This is your story. Tell it your way.
- Don't be afraid of revising and refining your story as your knowledge expands or your perception changes.

---

# 7

# Mourning the Loss

Eventually reality set in. *I'm autistic.*

Not the happy "Yay! I'm different! I'm unique! I'm special!" autistic.

More like "Holy crap ... I'm defective .. disabled ... challenged . . . never going to get any better" autistic.

This was when the mourning began. Once the bright shiny new *this-explains-everything* stage wore off, I started thinking about the other side of being autistic. I wasn't going to "outgrow" my social awkwardness. I wasn't going to wake up one day and suddenly have a balanced emotional life. The challenges I faced weren't imagined and they weren't going to magically disappear. They were with me for life.

This is me. This is always going to be me. Forever.

Talk about hard realizations.

The questions that arose were mostly variations of "how would my life have been different if I wasn't autistic?" As I tried to envision taking away this or that autistic part of me, it became obvious that Asperger's was responsible for a lot more than what makes me weird. It's responsible for many of my strengths, too. Take it away and I'm no longer me.

That person I was mourning? She doesn't exist.

## Mourning the Loss

---

- Don't be afraid to acknowledge your anger, disappointment, sadness or other negative feelings.
- Recognize your strengths along with your weaknesses.
- You've always been autistic and always will be. However, that doesn't mean you can't work on learning social skills, developing coping mechanisms or changing your lifestyle/environment in ways that support you.

---

# 8

# Healing the Child (or Younger Self)

Growing up undiagnosed is hard. There is a lot of pain that comes from knowing that you're different but not knowing why. Asperger's gave me an explanation, but more importantly it gave me a starting point for healing that scared, confused kid inside me.

As I worked back through the more difficult aspects of my childhood, I felt like I was somehow mothering my younger self—revisiting each moment, looking at it in a new light and telling that younger version of me that it wasn't my fault, that I'd done the best I could, that to expect more from me in the absence of support would have been unreasonable.

I wasn't "obviously" autistic as a child—girls manifest ASD traits differently than boys in many cases and Asperger's didn't exist as a diagnosis in the 1970s. The only children being diagnosed as autistic when I was a child were those with impairments significant enough to require round-the-clock care or specialized schooling.

I was, however, a handful. I was overly smart, easily bored, very curious and constantly in motion.

Consequently, I got a lot of guidance from adults on how to behave properly. This reined in my more problematic behaviors, but it also made me feel like I was forever in danger of doing something "wrong," especially when I "wasn't trying hard enough."

Being able to look back at my childhood and see that my behaviors were a result of my **brain chemistry** and not a result of "not being good enough" allowed me to begin to heal some of those lingering insecurities.

Learning more about Asperger's helped me understand that I was bullied not because I was weird, but because I was socially inept. Reading about selective mutism gave me an explanation for my largely silent elementary school years—the ones where I never spoke in class unless forced to. Finding information about how ASDs manifest in girls shed light on why I had so much trouble maintaining friendships.

Each new bit of information absolved me of some perceived failure as a child and helped me begin healing some very old wounds.

## Healing

---

- Learning more about ASD in children can help you understand challenges you faced in childhood.
- As an adult, you can choose to forgive the people in your life who hurt you as a child.
- It may help to imagine your adult self sharing your new information with your child self as a way to offer comfort or explanations for unhealed childhood wounds.
- If you find yourself having distressing reactions that are difficult to cope with, consult with a mental health professional or a trusted friend/mentor for help.

---

# 9

# Seeking a Diagnosis or Not

Whether you choose to seek a diagnosis or not is a personal decision. As an adult, there's a good chance you don't *need* a diagnosis. You may decide that you've done your research, come to the conclusion that you're on the spectrum and that's good enough for you.

This is commonly known as self-diagnosis and when done correctly, it's largely a well-respected approach among other adults in the ASD community. The primary reason? Getting an official diagnosis as an adult is difficult:

- Autism spectrum disorder presents differently in adults than in children. Finding someone in your area who is trained and experienced in adult diagnosis can be challenging.
- Many adults face numerous misdiagnoses before getting correctly diagnosed with Asperger's or autism.
- Women in particular are often misdiagnosed because they present differently than males,

on whom the traditional models of autism and Asperger's syndrome were based.

- Diagnosis can be expensive and an adult assessment isn't covered by most health insurance.
- Diagnosis can lead to bias, stigma and/or create practical limitations, like not being able to join the military or having your parental rights questioned.

Additionally, it's worth pointing out that many people self-diagnose before seeking out a professional diagnosis. This was the course I took. If I hadn't been relatively sure that I was on the spectrum, I don't think I could have justified investing the money, time and effort that it took to get professionally diagnosed.

### Self-diagnosis: A Framework for Self-discovery

How does self-diagnosis work? First, be prepared to do some work. Self-diagnosis isn't as simple as taking the AQ and deciding you're an aspie. Screening questionnaires or checklists like the one at the beginning of this guide can be a good place to start, but they're just that: a first step.

Here are some additional steps you can take to verify, challenge or test out your belief/suspicion that you're on the spectrum:

- Look at the DSM and/or ICD criteria for ASD (including DSM-IV-TR criteria for

Asperger's syndrome[1] and DSM-IV criteria for ASD[2], DSM-5 criteria for ASD are not yet available online, see Chapter 2 for a summary, ICD-10 criteria for Asperger's and ASD[3]).

- Review the list of symptom-based questions in Chapter 2 to help you identify common ASD traits in yourself.

- Be sure you understand what each of the diagnostic criteria means. ASD criteria manifest differently in adults than in children, so be sure to use examples of adult traits when considering whether each of the diagnostic criteria applies to you. It may also be helpful to think back to your childhood and try to determine whether you met the early signs of autism.[4]

- Read books on the subject, both nonfiction (like *The Complete Guide to Asperger's Syndrome*) and personal narratives (like *Pretending to Be Normal* or *The Journal of Best Practices*).

- Read about the experiences of Autistic adults; there are quite a few good blogs and books written by Autistic writers. If possible, talk with one or more Autistic adults. Comparing experiences with diagnosed adults can be

---

1 http://www.autreat.com/dsm4-aspergers.html

2 http://www.autreat.com/dsm4-autism.html

3 http://www.niccy.org/uploaded_docs/Aspergers%20Report/Appendix_1.pdf

4 http://www.cdc.gov/ncbddd/autism/signs.html

validating. Also, there are many Autistic adults online (on Tumblr, Twitter, Facebook, and blogs) who are happy to answer questions about specific aspects of autism and being autistic. Just keep in mind that Autistic adults are people too and we have a broad range of opinions as well as differing comfort levels when it comes to sharing our personal experiences.

- Make a realistic self-assessment of your autistic traits based on your reading.

- Talk with one or more trusted persons in your life about your self-assessment. Do they see the same traits that you've identified? Share a list of ASD traits[5] (or female ASD traits[6]) or the list of questions in Chapter 2 with them. Do they see traits that you haven't considered? Some things, like facial expressions and body language, are easier for other people to see in us than for us to perceive in ourselves.

- If you have access to childhood materials like report cards, school work, a baby book or old home movies/videos, review them in light of the childhood symptoms of AS/autism.

- If possible (and if you feel comfortable) ask your parents about your childhood. If you don't want to frame your questions in terms

---

5   http://www.help4aspergers.com/pb/wp_4a3112c8/wp_4a3112c8.html
6   You can find this list at (http://www.help4aspergers.com/pb/wp_a58d4f6a/images/img244154ad237783e339.JPG) or by searching online for "Rudy Simone list of female asperger traits"

of autistic symptoms, you could simply ask things like "Did my teachers say I [did X or behaved like Y]?" or "Do you remember me doing [X, Y or Z] when I was a toddler?"

As you do your research, keep in mind that not everyone has every symptom. Symptoms can change in severity and presentation over a lifetime, becoming either more or less noticeable with age. In fact, it's not unusual to find that as you age, one trait (like sensory sensitivities) becomes more manageable while another (like executive dysfunction) increases in severity. There also may be times when a symptom seems to disappear for awhile, only to return full-blown years later due to a change in circumstances or environment.

By the time you've completed your research, you should have an idea of whether autism spectrum disorder is a good fit for you. Many adults are content with this and choose to self-identify as aspie or autistic based on their self-discovery process. Others feel the need (or have a specific reason) to seek out a professional diagnosis, which can be a long and difficult journey.

Even if you choose to pursue a professional diagnosis, it's a good idea to work through the self-discovery process first. Often, getting diagnosed as an adult requires making a solid case for why you think an autism diagnosis fits you.

## Weighing Self- vs. Professional Diagnosis

---

- Obtaining a diagnosis as an adult can be very difficult.
- Not everyone needs or wants a professional diagnosis.
- Self-diagnosis is widely accepted in the autistic adult community when done with diligence.
- Self-discovery is a good first step toward professional diagnosis if you choose to pursue it.

---

# 10

# Obtaining a Formal Assessment

There are a number of reasons that an adult might want to seek out a diagnosis by a professional:

1. To become eligible for services
2. To obtain supports or accommodations at work or school
3. To increase the likelihood that therapy or counseling takes ASD traits into account
4. For peace of mind and/or validation of a self-diagnosis

Primarily, I fell into the last category. I needed to know that it wasn't "all in my head." Getting a diagnosis from a professional seemed like the most conclusive way to do that. However, if I ever go to graduate school (or have to get a job—I've been self-employed all my life), I like the idea of having an official diagnosis to back up any requests for supports that I might choose to make.

How do you go about getting evaluated for autism spectrum disorder as an adult? First, be prepared to face some significant challenges:

- You'll need to find a psychologist, psychiatrist or neuropsychologist who does adult ASD assessments. Depending on where you live, this task ranges from difficult to nearly impossible.
- You'll probably have to pay for the assessment yourself. Most insurance companies in the US don't cover adult ASD assessment. Be forewarned, a full assessment can cost anywhere from $1500 to $3000. I'll talk about other, potentially less costly options below.
- The process of getting diagnosed may take months or years and you may encounter misdiagnoses and misinformation along the way.

With all of the discouraging stuff out of the way, let's look at some of the options for getting diagnosed:

A good place to start if you're in the US is the Pathfinders for Autism Providers Directory.[1] Plug in your zip code, how far you're willing to travel (further will give you more options—I chose 50 miles when I did my search) and select the "Getting Diagnosed" option in the Categories list on the right.

You'll be given a (hopefully) long list of results to comb through, including psychologists, psychiatrists,

---

1  http://www.pathfindersforautism.org/providers

neuropsychologists and licensed clinical social workers. I know of people who have been diagnosed with ASD by all of these types of professionals except the last. Read the provider descriptions, visit their websites and/or call providers to narrow down your results to those who do adult assessments.

Other options for finding providers who do adult autism assessments:

- **Word of mouth**: If you can locate autistic individuals or parents of autistic children in your area, ask them for referrals.
- **State, provincial or local autism group**: Google "[your state/county/province/ major city] autism services" and look for .org website addresses in the results. You should find at least one local nonprofit or community autism services organization in your area. Call and request a referral for an adult assessment. If you find more than one, call all of them. Different organizations have different missions and their resource lists vary. You can also find a good but not exhaustive list of state-by-state resources on the GRASP website.[2]
- **Local university**: Call the medical school or teaching hospital for a large public university in your area and speak with someone in the neurology department. You may get

---

2 http://grasp.org/page/statebystate-help

transferred around a lot and have to explain your question repeatedly but this can be a way to find an adult specialist if you're coming up empty in other places.

Surprisingly, one source that probably won't be helpful is your primary care physician. I explained my concerns to my doctor and his reply was to offer to write me a prescription for a beta blocker for anxiety. When I turned that down, he suggested counseling.

What he didn't suggest was that I get evaluated for ASD. His approach was focused on treating the symptoms; he seemed to think the source of the symptoms was irrelevant. That's not to say he's a bad doctor. He probably wasn't trained to handle this type of question. Autism is still seen by many in the medical field as a childhood disease.

If you live outside the United States or if your insurance covers ASD assessment, a referral from a primary care doctor might be required to qualify for insurance coverage (or rebates or whatever form subsidized health care takes in your country). In this situation, you may need to approach your doctor armed with information about adult autism.

This is where your discovery process and perhaps self-diagnosis will come in handy. While there is increasing awareness of the existence of undiagnosed autistic adults, many primary care doctors aren't well informed about the subject. You may find that you're more knowledgeable than your doctor. Don't be afraid of advocating hard for a referral.

## Alternatives to a Formal Assessment

If the cost of a formal assessment is prohibitive, there are other options to consider:

1. Your community autism services organization may have a staff or consulting psychologist who evaluates adults for ASD. Depending on your financial situation, they may offer this service at reduced cost or as part of their services to the community.
2. Some universities with teaching hospitals or clinical centers offer ASD assessment conducted by supervised graduate students on an ability-to-pay basis.
3. You may be able to obtain a diagnosis as part of ongoing therapy with a psychologist or psychiatrist. Sometimes a therapist will raise the possibility of ASD or be willing to commit to a diagnosis on the basis of information you share during therapy sessions.
4. If you get a referral to a psychiatrist or neuropsychologist for a differential diagnosis for a covered condition (ADHD evaluation for adults is often covered by insurance) and the evaluator also evaluates you for ASD at the same time, it may be covered by your insurance.

## Finding the Right Provider

After doing extensive research, including everything listed above plus some fruitless things not included here, I came up with exactly two potential providers within a 50-mile radius of my major metropolitan city.

Armed with my very short list, I called the first provider—a psychiatrist whose name I'd obtained from a major university. This didn't go as well as I'd hoped. The doctor was extremely condescending and basically said, "Adult autism assessment is really expensive and I doubt you can afford it and why do you want it anyway?"

I gave a brief stuttering answer, hung up the phone shaking, and spent two weeks working up the courage to call the second and only other name on my list.

The second provider was a private neuropsychology practice specializing in cognitive testing for children and adults (primarily ADHD and ASD). To my great relief, the person who answered the phone didn't act like it was strange that I was calling to schedule an assessment for myself without any sort of referral. She didn't treat me like an idiot or become impatient with my questions.

I gathered the information about the testing process and said I'd call back after thinking about it. The assessment was going to be a big investment and taking that final step was intimidating. Bizarrely, my biggest fear was that the tests would prove I didn't have Asperger's or that the psychologist would think I wasn't autistic enough to merit a diagnosis. Then I'd be back to having no explanation for all the atypical things about me.

After a couple of days of thinking it over, I decided I definitely wanted to go forward. My husband was supportive of my decision and offered to come with me to the appointment if I wanted him to. I didn't take him up on the offer, but it felt good to know that he was 100% behind me.

Whatever path you take to finding someone who can evaluate you, know that it won't likely be a direct route. It's okay to feel like the biggest first step you can manage is to bring up a list of results on the Pathfinders website. Maybe your next step is reading about the providers and a few days later you might gather the energy to start making a list of providers to call. It may take weeks or months to start making those calls and yet more months to commit to meeting with a professional or scheduling an assessment.

Take your time. Ask for support from a trusted person in your life if you feel comfortable doing so. Getting diagnosed can be an uphill climb. Pace yourself.

## Finding a Professional who Works with Adults

---

- Be prepared to do a lot of research.
- Look for psychologists, psychiatrists or neuropsychologists who are experienced in diagnosing adults with ASD.
- If you have to get a referral from a primary care doctor, be prepared to advocate for yourself.
- If the cost of diagnosis is prohibitive, look for alternatives to private providers.
- Be patient and go forward at your own pace.

---

# 11

# Types of Assessments

There is no medical (genetic, blood, neuroimaging) test for autism. In fact there isn't even a single definitive method that professionals use to make a diagnosis, particularly for adults. All psychologists, psychiatrists and neuropsychologists follow the diagnostic criteria set out by the current DSM or ICD manual, but the processes they use for arriving at a diagnosis are varied.

Generally a diagnosis is made based on behavior—how you present, your answers to autism-related questions and your developmental history (if it's available). As part of your ASD assessment, you may talk with a psychologist or psychiatrist, take written or computer-based tests and/or complete questionnaires. You may also be asked to bring along a friend or family member who can provide details about your childhood and/or your day-to-day life. Finally, the evaluator will observe you during your visit(s) for signs of autistic traits.

The evaluator will focus primarily on behavior in two areas: social communication and restricted/repetitive behaviors. Within each area, he or she will be looking for specific traits, such as those described in the questions in Chapter 2. Depending on the type of assessment, it might be completed in a single visit or over the course of several visits.

You may receive a verbal diagnosis at the end of your assessment or you may have to wait until the evaluator has created a formal written report. In my case, I received a verbal diagnosis at my follow-up appointment several weeks after the assessment and then a detailed written report two weeks after that.

The goal of the assessment should be **not only to make or rule out a diagnosis of autism spectrum disorder, but to quantify your strengths and identify areas where you would benefit from supports and adaptations**. The evaluator may also make recommendations for psychotherapy, medication for co-occurring conditions (depression, anxiety, OCD) social skills training, job coaching or other steps you can take to address areas of concern.

Keep in mind that adult autism assessments are different than those typically done for children, which can involve several different professionals (child psychologist or psychiatrist, speech therapist, occupational therapist, audiologist, autism specialist, etc.). Most adult assessments are done by one or two professionals working out of the same office or facility.

## Types of Adult Assessments

1. **Assessment by a neuropsychologist**: Neuropsychologists use a combination of cognitive testing, questionnaires and diagnostic interview. The assessment can take up to eight or more hours depending on the number of tests and the pace that is comfortable for the person being evaluated.

2. **Assessment by a psychiatrist**: Psychiatrists often use a similar approach to neuropsychologists but may also use the approach described below in number 3. In either case, you may be asked to come in for a short preliminary visit where the doctor will prescreen you for ASD. This is sometimes done to verify that a full assessment is necessary. The cost for the preliminary screening should be in line with a typical office visit for the type of doctor you're seeing.

3. **Dedicated assessment by a psychologist**: If you are referred to or visit a psychologist specifically due to concerns that you might have autism spectrum disorder, the assessment will likely consist of a combination of symptom-based questionnaires and diagnostic interview sessions in which the psychologist will ask you about your symptoms, your history and your day-to-day functioning.

4. **Assessment by a psychologist in the course of therapy**: Sometimes the possibility of an

ASD diagnosis will be raised by a psychologist during the course of therapy for other issues. Some psychologists are willing to make a formal diagnosis in this context, while others are not. Part of the assessment in this situation may include completing questionnaires and/or a diagnostic interview.

5. **Assessment by a specialist after referral by a primary care physician**: In some circumstances (depending on your location or insurance coverage) you may be required to get a referral from your primary care physician in order to qualify for partial or full reimbursement of the cost of your assessment. In this case, your primary care physician may give you a screening questionnaire to complete (such as the AQ or AQ-10). He or she may also order medical tests to rule out other causes of symptoms you're experiencing. You may have to make more than one visit before getting a referral to someone specializing in autism assessment or you may get a referral on the spot. It's also possible that your physician will ask you if you prefer to be referred to a specific provider, so doing your homework on the specialists in your area in advance can be beneficial.

6. **Assessment by a trained assessor in a clinical setting**: If your assessment is done in a clinical setting (e. g., nonprofit autism services provider) it may be conducted by one or more trained assessors such as a graduate student, masters-

level psychology major and/or licensed clinical social worker. In this case, you may be seen by a team of people with different specialities. The assessment will likely focus on the diagnostic interview and screening questionnaires but may also include some cognitive testing.

Whatever form an assessment takes, it should ultimately be geared toward collecting the information necessary to determine whether you meet the diagnostic criteria for autism spectrum disorder, perhaps while ruling out other conditions.

## Paths to Diagnosis

- There is no medical test for autism.
- The format of adult ASD assessments varies by provider.
- Adult ASD assessments are different from those used to evaluate children.
- An assessment should result in both a diagnosis and a summary of your strengths and needs as well as recommendations for next steps.

# 12

# Preparing for Your ASD Assessment

My assessment was done by a neuropsychologist, so I'm going to talk about that in detail in this section to give you an in-depth idea of what an assessment using a diagnostic interview, cognitive testing, behavioral observation and symptom-related questionnaires is like. As I mentioned previously, an adult assessment may use some or all of these methods.

Neuropsychology is a field that looks at behavior in terms of brain function. Autism is a developmental disorder, not a mental illness, so diagnosing ASD is one of the areas that neuropsychologists specialize in. Clinical psychologists and psychiatrists who work with autistic patients will also use many of the same tests and procedures described here.

When I made my initial appointment, I was told that testing would take 4-8 hours and might be split over two or more appointments, depending on how fatiguing I found the tests.

A few days later I received a 17-page

questionnaire in the mail. The instructions said to complete it and bring it to my assessment. The questionnaire covered personal and family mental health history, cognitive symptoms (memory, daily function, auditory/visual/balance, etc.), childhood development and an open-ended question about why I was seeking an assessment.

I used the open-ended question to make my case. I started out with "I suspect I have Asperger's Syndrome" and then listed my major symptoms as I understood them at the time: social awkwardness, rigidity, attachment to routine, intense interests, difficulty reading facial expressions and body language, clumsiness, etc. I tried to focus on the symptoms that fit the DSM categories first and then listed other less universally recognized symptoms after that.

Beneath the open-ended question was a set of checkboxes that said:

```
Overall I think that there is:
   □ nothing wrong with me
   □ probably something wrong with me
   □ definitely something wrong with me
```

In true aspie fashion I checked the "definitely" box, crossed out "wrong," wrote in "**different**," then annotated it with a few descriptive sentences. In fact, I annotated a lot of the "ticky box" questions. By the time I was done, my questionnaire was a scribbled-on mess.

Whether you receive a history questionnaire or not, I strongly recommend making notes to bring to your appointment. The time you'll spend with the doctor conducting your assessment will be limited; it's important to bring up everything you think will be helpful in getting an accurate diagnosis.

If you find speaking about your symptoms difficult, prepare a concise (no more than 1 page) written summary to give to the doctor at the start of your appointment. Autism causes communication difficulties. There's nothing wrong with telling the doctor that you prefer to use a brief written description of your concerns as a starting point.

Most importantly, as you prepare for the appointment, try to relax. I know it feels like there's a lot riding on the outcome, but all you have to do at the appointment is **be yourself**. This is one time when being your own hot mess of an autistic self is encouraged.

## Preparing for Your Assessment

---

- If the provider sends you a history and/or symptom questionnaire, take it seriously. Fill it out as completely as possible, providing specific examples where you can. Don't hesitate to add additional information that you feel is relevant.
- Make notes regarding what you want to talk about as part of your diagnostic interview.
- If necessary, prepare a written summary of your symptoms/signs/traits for the doctor.
- If you have questions, write them down and bring them to the appointment so you don't forget.
- Try to relax and remember to be yourself.

---

# 13

# What an Adult ASD Assessment Consists of

The morning of my appointment, I was incredibly nervous. My biggest fear was that I would go through this process and be told that I was officially *not autistic*—that I wouldn't come across as "autistic enough" for a clinical diagnosis.

Fortunately, it turned out that I'd found a doctor who had worked with enough autistic adults to know that we have many coping mechanisms and workarounds. He didn't expect me to present the way a five-year-old boy would. He acknowledged that being an autistic adult doesn't necessarily mean not attending your cousin's baby shower; it can mean going to the baby shower and spending a good part of the afternoon hiding out in the kitchen (one of his examples).

## The Diagnostic Interview

The first part of my assessment was a diagnostic interview. I turned in my questionnaire to the receptionist and when Dr. H called me into his office, he'd obviously reviewed it. He started off by asking me to talk about why I suspected I have Asperger's. I was nervous, so I rambled around a lot. Looking back, I probably should have looked at my notes and used them as a guide, but my mind was going a hundred miles an hour.

Once my initial thoughts fizzled out, Dr. H. started working through the questionnaire, confirming symptoms I'd answered positively and asking clarifying questions. As I relaxed a little, the conversation became less structured. We talked a lot about my childhood, with the doctor encouraging me to give examples or tell stories to illustrate certain points. Gradually, he began inserting comments about Asperger's, explaining how some of my symptoms were typical and how they fit into the diagnostic picture.

The interview lasted about an hour. By the end of it, I felt like we'd hit on all of the key points I wanted to talk about as well as some that I hadn't considered. Dr. H concluded the interview by explaining that he wanted to evaluate me for ASD, ADHD and Social Anxiety Disorder. The second one was a surprise but I was glad that he was forming his own hypotheses in addition to the one I'd presented.

He then explained a little about how cognitive testing works and about the qualifications of B, the

ASD testing specialist who would administer the tests.

When we moved to B's office, I got a chance to demonstrate two of the traits I'd described in the interview: face blindness and delayed auditory processing. Dr. H introduced me to B and she cheerfully said, "Yes, we already met—you asked me where the restroom was when you came in."

Completely thrown by the fact that I didn't recognize her, I said "Really? Okay."

As I was kicking myself for that useless reply, Dr. H asked, "Got plurdled gabbleblotchits on a lurgid zoo?"

I reflexively replied, as I always do when I have no idea what someone has said, "Sorry?"

"What would you like to be called?" he repeated.

I probably could have gone home at that point because not recognizing that I'd already met B, not being able to smooth over the awkwardness that followed, not greeting her with my name, not understanding what Dr. H was saying, being more focused on orienting myself in the room than connecting with the person I was going to work with—in less than 60 seconds, I'd exhibited a boatload classic autistic behavior, much of it as a result of struggling to transition between activities and environments, which is in itself a textbook symptom of ASD.

To her credit, B quickly put me at ease. She spent about ten minutes "getting ready" while I sat, mostly silent, and studied the colorful barcode prints on her wall. Honestly, I think the time she spent puttering around with her supplies was more for my benefit than hers. By the time we started on the cognitive testing, I was feeling reasonably focused again.

## Cognitive Testing

Cognitive testing for ASD is a mix of verbal and nonverbal tests.

Some I found easy; others were a challenge. One actually made me bang my head on the desk, though I stopped as soon as I realized I was doing it because . . . inappropriate. Most of the tests were designed to start out easy and scale up in difficulty so that the last few were very challenging.

If you're planning to be evaluated, you may or may not want to read about the tests I took in detail. Consider this your spoiler warning: Skip to Chapter 14 now if you don't want detailed descriptions of the tests and the strategies I used on them.

Here is a list of the tests I took with a short description of each:

**WAIS-IV (full)**: An adult IQ test that measures verbal comprehension, perceptual reasoning, working memory and processing speed.

- The **verbal** portion covered things like describing the similarities between two words (i.e. anchor and fence, statue and poem, allow and restrict), defining vocabulary words and answering general information questions. I found the "similarities" test challenging because some of the pairs had conceptual rather than concrete similarities. The other two sections were fairly easy because I'm both a walking dictionary and an encyclopedia of random facts.

- The **perceptual reasoning** portion was a series of visual puzzles: using colored blocks to reproduce a design, deducing which design comes next in a series, and choosing shapes to form a larger shape. These tests were fun, although I found myself guessing at times.

- The **working memory** tests involved repeating back strings of digits in forward and reverse order and doing math problems verbally. By the end of the digit string tests I was rocking back and forth in my chair with my eyes closed tight. The math problems, on the other hand, were fun. This set of tests made me conscious of how much I talk out loud to myself when my brain is working hard.

- The **processing speed** portion involved locating symbols and coding a series of numbers into symbols. These were both fairly straight-forward pattern recognition tests that required balancing speed and accuracy.

**Woodcock-Johnson III (partial)**: A test of academic skills that included orally identifying written words, orally spelling words given by oral prompt, and doing some paper and pencil math problems, ranging from pre-algebra to basic calculus.

I got tripped up by the word "questionnaire" on the spelling test. It's one of those words that I always use autocorrect on. There is no autocorrect on an oral spelling test.

**Wechsler Memory Scale IV (partial)**: The portion of this test that I took tested auditory memory. It involved two parts:

- listening to a brief factual story and retelling it, including as many facts as possible, then responding with true/false answers to factual questions about the story (two trials)
- listening to a long list of word pairs and then responding to a word prompt with the correct paired word (interminable number of trials)

I struggled mightily with both of these. My working memory is poor, especially when working verbally under pressure.

**Word Fluency**: A timed test in which I had to think of as many words as possible that fit the following categories: animals, words starting with A, words starting with F, and words starting with S. These were challenging—I started out with a good head of steam but once I lost my momentum, I started perseverating on the words I'd already named instead of thinking of new words. Until I realized that I could name things in the room that fit the prompt. Aspie adaptation for the win.

**Rey-Osterrieth Complex Figure Test**: A measure of organization and planning skills as well as fine motor skills. It involves reproducing a complex drawing (shown below) using a series of colored pencils that allow the evaluator to track the order in which the figure was drawn as well as the accuracy of reproduction.

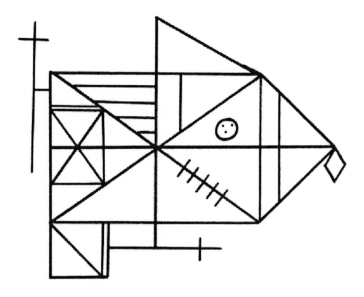

Thirty minutes later, without any warning, I was asked to reproduce the same figure from memory. This did not go well. What I managed to reproduce the second time was basically a box with an X through it, a flag sticking out the front and bowling ball floating in the upper right corner. Bizarrely, I still remember exactly what it looked like and could draw *that* from memory months later.

**California Verbal Learning Test**: Another test involving recalling items from a list with multiple trials. Again, I struggled. The correct strategy, which I realized on the fourth trial, was to chunk the words by category to make recalling them easier. There were only five or six trials, so my realization came kind of late to be useful. This test also had me closing my eyes and talking to myself out loud because I was so frustrated with how difficult it was. There might have been some cursing. I was getting tired.

**Trailmaking Test**: A connect-the-dots type of test, first connecting numbers only and then connecting an alternating sequence of numbers and letters. This measures visual scanning and sequencing ability. Surprisingly, I was quicker at the second series, even though it was the more difficult task.

**Stroop Color and Word Test**: A series of three visual to verbal tests:

- verbally reading off a list of color words (blue, red, green) printed in black ink
- verbally giving the color of a series of Xs which were printed in blue, red or green ink
- verbally reading a list of color words, with each printed in a different color ink (i.e. "red" printed in blue ink)

This test was deceptively easy. So much so, that when I saw my results, I was shocked. I scored in the "impaired" range on the first two and in the "high average" range on the third (and hardest) test.

Performing better on the more challenging versions of the Stroop and trailmaking tests leads me to believe that I'm more motivated to perform accurately on challenging tasks and if a task is too simple, I get bored and easily distracted.

## Other Neuropsychological Tests

**Grooved Pegboard Test**: A timed test of fine motor skills that consists of putting small metal pegs in a pegboard, first with the right hand and then with the left. The only problem I had with this one was accidentally switching back to the right-handed order of inserting the pegs (right-to-left) when I was doing the left-handed test (meant to be completed left-to-right).

**Reciprocal Motor Programs Test**: A test of how well I could repeat and then reverse-repeat a series of finger taps.

## ADHD Test

**IVA Continuous Performance Test**: This was the only cognitive test conducted by computer. The computer provided visual and auditory prompts at random intervals. If the prompt was a 1, I was supposed to click the mouse. If the prompt was a 2, I was supposed to refrain from clicking. The test was 21 minutes long. By the halfway point, I was stimming ferociously. I was also determined to ace this test (perhaps out of fear of being misdiagnosed with ADHD) so first I pretended that I was an air traffic controller and if I missed a cue, an airplane would crash. When that stopped working, I told myself that if I missed a cue, a puppy would die. Yeah, I take this stuff way too seriously. It took me awhile to wind down after this test was over because I sent myself into a state of extreme hyperfocus.

## Questionnaires

I also completed four self-report questionnaires:

**MCMI-III**: This consisted of 180 true-false questions that test for 14 personality disorders (e.g. schizoid, depressive, compulsive) and 10 clinical syndromes (e.g., anxiety, bipolar, PTSD). There were also some funny questions, like "I am currently in an airplane" meant to verify that I was paying attention. Or not delusional. Hard to say.

**Beck Depression Inventory (BDI-II)**: A 21-question self-report instrument for measuring the presence and severity of depression symptoms.

**Beck Anxiety Inventory (BAI)**: A 21-question self-report instrument for measuring the presence and severity of anxiety symptoms. The questions on this form made me realize that what I think if as anxiety and the clinical definition of anxiety are not the same thing. The clinical definition is much more serious and pervasive than what I experience.

**Current and Childhood ADHD self-report**: A self-report instrument for measuring the presence and severity of ADHD symptoms now and during childhood.

## Getting the Most Out of Your Assessment

---

- Bring your notes to the diagnostic interview appointment and don't be afraid to consult them.
- Try to use stories or specific examples when answering questions about symptoms or traits.
- Be yourself and answer as completely and honestly as possible.
- Keep in mind that what you share with the doctor is confidential and you don't need to feel embarrassed about or ashamed of your behavior or feelings.
- You may be given tests or questionnaires to rule out other conditions such as depression, anxiety, ADHD, OCD or schizophrenia. Complete everything to the best of your ability, even if you think the questions are not applicable to you.

---

# 14

## A Moment of Suspension

If you've read through the components of my ASD assessment, you might be wondering *but what about the Asperger's questionnaire?*

There wasn't one. I didn't complete a written screening or diagnostic test like the RAADS-R or AQ. My ASD diagnosis was based on the diagnostic interview, the outcomes of the cognitive/neuropsychological testing and behavioral observations made by Dr. H and B during my visit.

However, between the diagnostic interview and the behavioral observation, the key questions on the screening instruments were addressed in detail. The diagnostic interview covered questions on my special interests, relationships, social preferences, sensory sensitivities, attention, language pragmatics and fine motor skills. The behavioral observation included general presentation (grooming and dress), gait, speech (rhythm, rate and volume), demeanor, verbal skills, eye contact, movement patterns and conversation habits.

The interview and testing took about five and half hours. It was exhausting. We went straight through lunch, though both B and Dr. H told me that I could ask for a break at any time. The thing is, when I'm that engaged in something, I forget that I need to eat. I may be hungry, but the hunger signal gets muted.

So, exhausted and hungry, wishing I'd taken my husband up on his offer of a ride, I scheduled my follow-up appointment and stumbled out to the car. My assessment was done. In three weeks I'd have a diagnosis.

Or not.

A rising sense of panic settled in as I started rehashing every detail of the appointment. Worse, I knew that I had three weeks ahead of me to perseverate on what I'd said and done and not said and not done. Three weeks to wonder if I'd done "too well" on the cognitive tests, if I'd instinctively made an effort to pass for "normal" (as I so often do with strangers) in the interview, if I'd withheld key details or reflexively covered my weaknesses.

Three whole weeks to alternately tell myself that this had been the best and the worst thing I'd ever done for myself.

The days passed about as quickly as you'd expect. I was restless and unsettled, plagued by a string of nightmares. The idea that Asperger's might be something I'd talked myself into or imagined haunted me. My biggest fear—the one I couldn't shake—was that Dr. H would tell me I wasn't autistic, that in fact there was nothing wrong with me.

Then what? I'd found an explanation that fit so well. If someone "officially" took it away from me, I would be lost again, left to start over in search of a new, better explanation.

## Waiting for Answers

---

- After your assessment is complete, you may receive a verbal diagnosis right away or you may not be told anything about the results until a later appointment
- If there is a long interval between your assessment and follow-up appointments, try to distract yourself by planning activities you enjoy.
- If you have a trusted friend or mentor, talk to him or her about your assessment experience to help process your thoughts and feelings.

---

# 15

# The Follow Up Appointment

The day of the follow-up appointment finally arrived. As I rode the elevator up to the fourth floor, I felt my anxiety skyrocketing. I focused on breathing. I mentally rehearsed what I was going to say to the receptionist.

"I have a 2 o'clock appointment with Dr. H" isn't complex conversation, but when I'm at a DEFCON 1 anxiety level, I can forget my own name.

The ten minutes I spent sitting in the waiting room felt endless. I was contemplating a dash to the restroom when Dr. H poked his head around the corner and called me in.

If you want an example of how, er, unusual my conversation style can be when my social resources are low, this is the way our conversation began:

> Dr. H: "Good to see you again. What's new since you were here last time?"

> Me: "You rearranged your chairs."

Well, he had. The last time I visited, there was one guest chair facing his desk. Now there were three. That was not only new, it was messing with me, because I had to decide which one to sit in and none of the options was comfortable.

I settled on the middle chair and waited patiently while he made small talk about I have no idea what. Okay, semi-patiently. There was some discreet stimming happening. Maybe a lot.

Eventually—and I think the delay was him wanting to break it to me gently—he got around to telling me first how well I did on the cognitive testing and then that I'm clearly on the autism spectrum. I was relieved and yet somehow it felt unreal. For a moment I thought maybe I was dreaming because I'd been having a lot of dreams about the assessment and follow-up appointment.

My nonresponse confused him, I think. Over the course of our one-hour appointment, he asked me three times how I was feeling about the diagnosis. Each time, my reply was a variation of, "I guess I'm not that surprised." I thought I'd feel something more strongly, but I was too focused on the information he was giving me about my test results to have any real feelings.

Seeing my cognitive processes summed up in a neat table of numbers and percentiles was fascinating. I hadn't had a full IQ test since I was kid and back then no one would let me see the results.

Overall, the tests told me what I had suspected. My working memory, elements of executive functioning and verbal functioning are impaired. My nonverbal reasoning and verbal comprehension are significant strengths. The rest of my test scores fell in the average ranges.

I passed the ADHD test with flying colors, meaning that my distractibility is related to the poor executive function that is a hallmark of ASD. This wasn't a surprise; my attention problems are situational rather than across the board.

The tests also illustrate how it's possible for me to be both very literate and not very verbal. I scored highly on comprehension, spelling and vocabulary—which are receptive language skills or the ability to understand and process incoming words. I scored poorly on visual to verbal tasks (translating written words into speech), verbal working memory (remembering and repeating back spoken words) and verbal fluency (describing or listing words verbally). Those are all expressive language skills.

There is definitely faulty wiring between my thought and my speech. On the cognitive tests, that manifested as a measurable  discrepancy between my receptive and expressive language capacity. It feels good to have concrete evidence.

You'll often hear that ASD is associated with an uneven or spiky cognitive profile. While everyone has some variation in their cognitive abilities, the variation tends to be within a particular band (i.e., clustered around the 70th and 80th percentiles) rather than widely dispersed.

To give you an idea of how dramatically disparate the cognitive abilities of autistic individuals can be, I had a bunch of scores in the 98th and 99th percentiles, but I also had a cluster that included the 8th, 10th and 12th percentile. I am simultaneously off-the-charts extraordinary and bottom-of-the-barrel impaired. In yet other areas, I'm perfectly average.

One thing that really struck me in reading about spiky cognitive profiles and autism is that a profile like mine (nonverbal > verbal) is more strongly associated with impaired social skills than the reverse profile. It's also interesting to note that the dissociation between nonverbal and verbal abilities grows more significant with age, beginning very early in childhood.

After reviewing the test results and confirming that I was okay with my diagnosis, Dr. H emphasized that he was most concerned about my social anxiety and felt that counseling would help me cope better with my daily life. He gave me a referral to a counselor experienced in working with autistic adults and I agreed to think about it.

It took awhile for my diagnosis to sink in. At first, it didn't feel real. In a way, I'd known for a while that I was an aspie. Dr. H even jokingly said at one point toward the end of our follow-up appointment, "You made a good diagnosis, doctor."

In the days that followed, I slowly started to feel the peace of mind that I'd been craving settle in. By the time I received the written report on my tests, with it's official looking diagnostic conclusions, I finally felt some closure.

## Getting the Results of Your Assessment

---

- Your reaction to receiving a diagnosis may be relief, disbelief, sadness, anger, or nothing at all. That's okay.

- The outcome of your assessment may be different from what you expected. If you think the doctor has misdiagnosed you, don't be afraid to raise this possibility at the follow-up appointment.

- If you have questions about any aspects of your diagnosis, the follow-up appointment is the best time to ask them, while your assessment is still fresh in your doctor's mind.

- If you need post-diagnostic support, ask your doctor for a referral.

- If your doctor provides referral information, take it, whether or not you think you want to see a doctor or counselor. You may change your mind later, and if you do, you'll have a referral on hand.

- You don't need to make any decisions about therapy, medication or other steps right away.

- Give yourself enough time to absorb your diagnosis and be kind to yourself as you do.

---

# 16

# Moving Forward

The decision to pursue a diagnosis was difficult to make. There were times when I doubted my choice. Was it necessary to have a professional diagnosis? Would it make a difference?

Having gone through the process, the answer to both questions is yes. I have a strong need for closure. I don't deal well with gray areas and uncertainty. That piece of paper that says, "299.80 Asperger's Syndrome" closes off an avenue of doubt for me.

It also allows me to say this: if you think you're an aspie or autistic—if you've done the research and talked to other people on the spectrum and see yourself in them, if you've identified a long list of autistic traits in yourself and come to the conclusion that ASD describes your particular set of neurological differences—then you are very likely correct. With or without an official-looking paper diagnosis, I think we are our own best judges of our neurology.

So, yes, getting diagnosed was worth the time, effort and expense for me. Yes, I'm fortunate to be in a position to have access to the resources I needed to pursue it. Yes, I also believe that self-diagnosis can be valid.

One of the reasons I've written in detail about the process is because I know that not everyone can afford or has access to a diagnosis. Not everyone is ready to pursue getting diagnosed. Not everyone has the executive function or the emotional resources to run the gauntlet of medical and mental health providers. Not everyone needs or wants a formal diagnosis.

But I think everyone who has bothered to read this far probably shares my interest in self-discovery. We know that we're different and we want to know why and how and what that means. I spent less than 8 hours with the people who diagnosed me, but I've spent hundreds and hundreds of hours researching and writing about being autistic. That, ultimately, is what matters most to me.

My diagnosis, though it allowed me to put one set of questions to bed, has raised plenty of others.

- Are there things in my life that I want to change?
- Should I go for therapy?
- Who should I tell?
- How?
- What does it mean to be Autistic?

These aren't questions I can answer conclusively, even today.

## Moving Forward After a Diagnosis

---

- The choice to pursue a professional diagnosis or not is a personal one. Do what you feel is right for you.
- You are the best expert on your own neurology.
- A diagnosis may provide closure but it is not the end of the journey and may raise as many questions as it answers.

---

# 17

# Time to Change?

Once the newness of the diagnosis began to wear off, I was faced with the question of what to do with this new knowledge. I have a 10-page report from the neuropsychologist listing my cognitive strengths and weaknesses. I've become more familiar with and conscious of the areas where I struggle.

I've been told, not for the first time, that therapy would be beneficial. It's an idea that I keep kicking to the back of the line, intent instead on rigorous self-examination. Slowly, I've been working at making specific changes. I've written on my blog (musingsofanaspie.com) about being more flexible, allowing myself to stim more, trying to reduce my insomnia and nightmares, learning to translate from aspie to neurotypical and back, and exploring my emotions.

I've also written about the things I've decided need accepting rather than changing: my anxiety, my tactile defensiveness, my love of being alone. My litmus test for change vs. acceptance is simple: is the cost of changing this thing higher than the benefit

I'll gain from the change?

Some changes require little more than mindfulness or occasional reminders; other changes require me to move out of my comfort zone and face some hard truths. The outcome—or at least the goal—is that I struggle less with some aspect of my life. Those are the good changes, the ones I'm eager to make.

Other changes feel pointless to me. These are often the changes that would make other people more comfortable by making me seem less odd. With all of the things I could be working on, I don't see the point of investing my limited energy in those types of changes.

In fact, since getting diagnosed, I've become more echolalic, more stim-y, less conscious of censoring myself. I've become gentler and more compassionate with myself. I push myself less; cut myself slack where I wouldn't have before. Not because I see myself as disabled, but because I see myself as a person in need of care.

I never really gave much thought to self-care before. I often demanded a level of performance and perfection from myself that I wouldn't have expected from another person. I was so busy pushing myself to be better, to get things right, that I often neglected to be kind to myself.

Perhaps that's the biggest change I've made so far: I've resolved to be kind to myself.

Obviously, these are very personal decisions. The constellation of things that I choose to work on changing is unique to me. It continues to shift and grow. There are days when I think, "screw this, why should I change anything?" There are days when I think it would be nice to be "normal" for a day, to not have to struggle so much with simple things.

Then there are days when being autistic recedes into the background, not because I'm less autistic, but because I'm more comfortably autistic. Little by little, I feel myself healing old wounds, integrating the shiny new realizations, and becoming more myself.

That's the best change of all.

Making Changes, Accepting Your Differences

---

- It's up to you to decide what you want to change and how. You're different not broken.
- Acceptance is as important as adaptation.
- Self-care is essential for everyone but especially for autistic adults. Make it a priority in your life.

---

# 18

# Disclosing Your ASD

Disclosure, it turns out, is a sticky issue. My first instinct was, "This is great! I have an explanation for my difficulties. I'll tell everyone and they'll be as happy about it as I am."

Er, no. Disclosure makes people uncomfortable. Most people don't know what to say. Many will reassure you that it makes no difference and then proceed to treat you differently. Even in the people who are very accepting, you may notice the occasional patronizing statement or doubt about your competence—little shifts in the way this person sees you now that you're autistic.

Not that you weren't autistic before, of course. But handing a label as loaded as autistic to another person changes things, like it or not.

## Who to Share Your Diagnosis With

Some autistic adults openly disclose to everyone. Others share only with close friends and/or family. Some people disclose in stages, starting with an inner circle and working outward as they feel more comfortable.

As you think about disclosure, keep one thing in mind: it's irrevocable. Once you share your news with someone, you can't unshare it. You also can't guarantee that the person you've shared with will keep your disclosure private. They may inadvertently or intentionally "out" you to someone you aren't ready to share with.

Still, many of the people in our lives already know that we're a little different. Generally, most people choose to share their diagnosis with the people closest to them. This might include immediate family, close friends and/or a significant other. If you prefer not to share beyond this inner circle of people, be sure to make it clear when disclosing that your diagnosis is private information.

Beyond your inner circle, it may become harder to decide who to share with. Obviously, you don't need to notify casual acquaintances but what about work colleagues, supervisors, professors or other people you interact with regularly?

It may help to consider the consequences of disclosing versus not disclosing. If you've only recently been diagnosed then you already have a good idea of what not disclosing looks like. Are you happy with the current situation? Would disclosing allow you to ask for needed supports or accommodations?

Is it possible that disclosing would create more risks than benefits?

There are real dangers to disclosure in some situations. You can open yourself to discrimination and bias, especially when it comes to work, school, or your parenting rights. I'm not writing this to frighten you. Just be sure you've done your homework and thought through the possible consequences before choosing to disclose your diagnosis. If you're unsure, consider talking with a trusted friend or mentor before making a decision.

## What to Say

There are two ways to go about disclosure. You can make a full disclosure, using the words *autistic, Asperger's syndrome* or *autism spectrum disorder.* If you decide to go this route, be prepared to do some education. There's a good chance the other person's first reaction will be "but you don't seem/look/act that autistic" or "I never would have guessed" or some other similarly awkward reply.

Preparing a short script describing autism as a neurological condition that impacts your communication, social interaction and sensory processing can be helpful. The operative word here is short. You don't need to give the person a TED talk on autism. Just share a few facts relevant to your situation, including what kind of accommodations or supports you are requesting.

If you aren't going to request accommodations, it's probably best not to disclose in a work situation, unless you're the kind of person who is confident with being out to everyone. Because of the stigma associated with ASD, the risks of workplace disclosure can be significant and irreparable.

There is always the possibility that disclosure will bring with it the subtle, hard-to-prove sort of discrimination that doesn't rise to the point of being actionable under law. Although autism falls under the purview of the Americans With Disabilities Act, human social interaction is unpredictable and fraught with gray areas.

You may be able to request accommodations or supports without using the word autism, if that feels safer. For example, if you have a job doing data entry in a noisy workspace, you can explain to your supervisor that wearing noise canceling headphones will enhance your concentration, making you more productive.

If this request is well received, you don't need to disclose your disability if you prefer not to. If it's not received well, you'll likely have to disclose that you're autistic to gain accommodations under the Americans With Disabilities Act (if you live in the United States—other countries have their own laws and requirements). It's a good idea to do some research about your rights and your employer's obligations under ADA[1] before proceeding. For example, here is a list of common types of accommodations.[2]

---

1    http://www.eeoc.gov/facts/ada18.html
2    http://www.eeoc.gov/eeoc/internal/reasonable_accommodation.cfm#1

While ADA provides a minimum set of rights and obligations, some disability-friendly workplaces may be willing to do more to accommodate employees. For example, there are job coaches who work with individual employees to provide guidance about job-related tasks, run interference with co-workers and provide department-wide workplace educational seminars on ASD. All of these services can smooth the transition into the workplace for an autistic employee and help ensure long-term success on the job.

On the other hand, be aware that small businesses (fewer than 15 employees) are not subject to ADA requirements. That doesn't mean that a small business won't be willing to work with you on accommodations, just that they aren't required to under US law.

### When to Disclose

There is one more caveat to the choice not to disclose. If you don't share information about your disability upfront, sharing it when you find yourself in a bind will probably not be helpful. For example, two months into a new job, your supervisor calls you into his office and says you're being put on probationary status due to poor performance. This is not the time to disclose that you're struggling and you really needed to get all of your instructions in writing or to have tasks broken down into smaller elements with more closely supervised due dates . . . because you have autism.

If you know you'll need accommodations to successfully complete work or school tasks, ask for them upfront. If you discover that you need accommodations in the course of doing a task, request them as soon as possible. Don't wait until you're on the verge of disaster. Doing so will be seen by most people as "using your disability as an excuse." Fair or not, that's how it will be perceived, possibly making it much harder to gain the needed accommodations or even to keep your job in the long run.

There is also a special situation in which you may need to unexpectedly disclose your condition: an emergency. Some autistic people carry a card or letter in their wallet briefly describing what ASD is and how it might affect their responses in an emergency situation. If you lose speech under stress, respond negatively to being touched by strangers, or have sensitivities to flashing lights or loud noises, that information can be especially helpful for law enforcement and other first responders. This type of disclosure can prevent police or emergency medical personnel from mistakenly thinking that you're drunk or intentionally uncooperative.

## How to Disclose

I'm going to step backward here a bit and address this to both those who are diagnosed and those who aren't: disclosure is something that I found taking place at all stages of the journey. In the very early days of learning about ASD, you may find yourself needing to talk about your suspicions or realizations with someone close to you. As you move through the self-discovery and diagnostic process, you may need to talk with family members to gather information about your childhood or confirm details about yourself.

Disclosure doesn't only happen after a diagnosis. It can take place in stages, along a continuum. So here are some suggestions that may apply during different stages of the process:

- Request a **formal meeting or schedule a conversation**. This signals that what you intend to say is important. A formal appointment is most appropriate for work and school related disclosures, but it's also good for situations where you're concerned that the other party may not take you seriously.
- Raise your diagnosis **informally in conversation**, when the opportunity arises. This approach is more appropriate for those you anticipate being supportive.
- **Share an article about ASD**. This is a good way to open the "does this sound like me?" conversation with someone close to you.
- **Send an email or letter** disclosing your diagnosis and sharing relevant background

information about ASD. Personalized written communication is good for disclosing to people you find hardest to tell, for example family members who you're concerned might have a critical reaction.

- Share a **form letter or informational flyer.** Less personal written materials are an efficient way to share key facts in situations like emergencies or when requesting accommodations from public places (like a theme park).

- **Enlist an ally.** If you're faced with an especially hard disclosure situation, an ally can help you deliver the news, answer questions and/ or offer moral support, especially if there's a chance you might become completely or partially nonverbal during the encounter.

### Why Are You Disclosing?

Ultimately, this is the most important question. Before you disclose to someone, ask yourself what you expect to happen. Are you disclosing to ask for accommodations or understanding? Are you seeking acceptance and support?

What if you don't get what you're seeking? Sadly, this is often the outcome. Disclosure is hard. It requires a certain amount of fortitude, not just for the act of disclosing but for standing up to all that follows in the wake of it. Think it through, go slowly and enlist support from trusted people in your life.

## The Fundamentals of Disclosure:

---

- Disclosure has consequences—positive and negative—and is irrevocable.
- Disclosure can take many forms: formal, informal, education, advocacy, etc.
- Plan your disclosure opportunities carefully, seeking advice or assistance from a trusted friend or mentor as needed.
- Know why you are disclosing and what your desired outcome is.
- Be aware of the potential for hidden or unintended consequences of disclosure, especially in the workplace.
- Know your legal rights and obligations.

---

# 19

# An Evolving Sense of Self

In addition to the new set of questions that my diagnosis raised, it's also forced me to think about my identity and how I want to own being autistic.

Recently, I've been using *autistic* and *aspie* interchangeably to refer to myself. Not because the DSM-V has eliminated Asperger's but because it feels more comfortable. I've also been learning about the social model of disability[1], which says that disability is created by the way society is organized rather than by a person's differences.

My previous concept of disability had centered on the medical model which says that people are disabled by their differences and that those differences need to be fixed. Because I was resistant to the idea of being seen as someone who is "less" or "defective" I was resistant to thinking of myself as disabled. The social model of disability has given me a much more positive way of thinking about disability. It looks at

---

1    http://www.scope.org.uk/about-us/our-brand/talking-about-disability/social-model-disability

a person's disability and asks what kind of supports that person needs, not what's wrong with them.

The social model feels like a good fit for Autistic people. I don't want to be fixed but there are some things that would make my life easier.

## Learning to be Autistic

Since I've begun writing about autism, I've noticed that I have a constantly evolving sense of self. The more I write and read and talk with other people, the more my understanding of who I am shifts and solidifies.

Little by little, I'm learning what it means to be autistic.

You may notice that I generally use "small a" autistic rather than "capital A" Autistic in my writing. That's intentional, not an oversight.

Autistic refers to Autistic people as a cultural group. For example, I consider my blog Autistic space--a safe space where Autistic people can gather to share information about how we experience the world. I make an effort to participate in Autistic advocacy events online, like flash blogs. But I don't feel ready yet to be an advocate in the sense that many other Autistic adults and teens are.

The funny thing is, I never thought about being an advocate at all until recently. I started writing as a way to process my huge new self-discovery. Writing has always been my primary way of processing. Big thing to process equals a need to write hundreds of thousands of words in response.

As I got involved in the online blogging community, I slowly began to realize that like it or not, I am an advocate. That's something that I've come to take very seriously. Words have consequences. We can lob them like rocks or wield them like a scalpel; we can use them to soothe or incite. Mostly I want to use them to understand and to promote acceptance--self-acceptance and acceptance of Autistic people in general.

I feel like I'm still learning to be autistic. This is personal for me right now. Perhaps this is my way of being an advocate--the constant dissecting and researching and writing.

At some point I'd like to also feel comfortably Autistic, but for now, discovering my "small a" autistic self is an all-consuming process.

### Integrating Your Identify as an Autistic Person:

---

- An ASD diagnosis can raise serious questions about how we identify.
- There are many models of disability and many ways of being autistic.
- Some autistic adults choose to be a part of Autistic culture or socialize in Autistic spaces as a way of finding community.
- If you've spent a great deal of your life not knowing that you are autistic, it may take time to learn what being autistic means on both personal and cultural levels.

---

# 20

# Closing Thoughts

Wherever you are in your journey, you're not alone. There are other adults out there with the same questions, the same confusion, the same doubts and fears, the same excitement and aha! moments. The realization that you might be autistic or the discovery that you are can be life altering.

As someone who has gone through the ups and downs of getting an ASD diagnosis as an adult, I can tell you that it changes everything and at the same time, I'm much the same person I was before. I have always been autistic and I always will be. The difference is now I'm struggling less with myself.

The self-knowledge that I've gained through the discovery and diagnosis process has helped me accept myself as I am and identify the types of changes I'd like to make in my life. Some changes have been easy and others feel impossible to pull off, but the process continues to teach me about myself in new and unexpected ways.

Wherever your own journey leads you, I wish you courage and perseverance and happiness.

## Acknowledgements

I would like to thank the readers of my blog who commented on parts of this as I wrote it. Their support, encouragement and input have been invaluable. I'm particularly grateful to Kathryn, Nat, Mados, Littleostow, Susan, Trudi, Adrienne and Georgia.

From the earliest realizations that I might be autistic and through all the steps of my search for answers, my daughter Jess has been my biggest cheerleader. Her unconditional acceptance, understanding and encouragement are something I'll always treasure.

I could write a book about all the ways my husband, Sang, has contributed to my journey. Instead, I'll simply say I wouldn't be the person I am today without him and for that I'm deeply grateful.

# Index